Illustrations by MATT KELLEY

The crazy daze of MOTHERHOOD

JANE ISFELD STILL

BONNEVILLE BOOKS
SPRINGVILLE, UTAH

ISBN 13: 978-1-59955-495-2

Published by Bonneville Books, an imprint of Cedar Fort, Inc., 2373 W. 700 S., Springville, UT, 84663
Distributed by Cedar Fort, Inc., www.cedarfort.com

LIBRARY OF CONGRESS CATALOGING-IN-PUBLICATION DATA

Still, Jane Isfeld, 1954–
Crazy daze of motherhood / written by Jane Isfeld Still ;
illustrated by Matt Kelley.
p. cm.
Summary: Humorous stories taken from the author's own life.
ISBN 978-1-59955-495-2
1. Humorous stories, American. 2. Motherhood--Humor. I. Title.

HQ759.S6943 2010
306.874'3092--dc22

2010041023

Illustrated by Matt Kelley
Cover and page design by Angela D. Olsen
Cover design © 2011 by Lyle Mortimer
Edited by Kelley Konzak

Printed in the United States of America

10 9 8 7 6 5 4 3 2 1

Printed on acid-free paper

Dedication

Dedicated to my writer's group

Charlotte Lindstrom, Melanee Evans, MaryAlice Wallis,

Terry Brandon, and Diane Pond

for being there when my book needed

some tender caring 911.

contents

Emergency Response Team

WHEN MY HUSBAND and I applied for our marriage license, we simply walked up to the clerk and paid our money. He handed us a little piece of paper and said, "Next."

That was it. There was no interrogation, no screening of any kind. No one asked me if I was an ambulance driver, a paramedic, a dog whisperer, a pest exterminator, a plumber, or an emergency responder of any other ilk; nor if I was ever likely to become one.

In college I trained in the quintessential art of shorthand. Not once, in my entire life, has there ever been a need, let alone an urgency, to use that skill. Never have I been faced with an emergency where I said, "Boy, is my shorthand coming in handy now."

It wasn't that I went into marriage completely inept. I had skills. I knew the importance of shaving my legs and under my arms, of applying makeup every day, and of generally trying to look and smell nice. This skill not only had attracted a husband but it also came in useful when I needed someone to change a flat tire.

College was not a complete waste of time, however; I did learn a little something about plumbing.

One day I walked into the bathroom and noticed a mountain of toilet paper in the toilet. Naturally, I flushed. As the water rose higher and higher, I began to worry. If I didn't do something fast, it was going to flood.

Why is the plunger never around when you need it? It's not like it has a multitude of uses. I have never yet seen it mistaken for a potato masher, and I would have noticed someone using it as an umbrella.

Without a plunger or plumber handy, there was only one logical thing to do. I closed the lid to the toilet and sat on it. I stuck my legs straight out in front of me to push the lid down harder.

It didn't work. Water surged out onto the floor. In a matter of moments, it was streaming toward the bedroom carpet. I was stunned, and my mind went blank for a moment before snapping into action.

This situation called for quick thinking and intelligence. I jumped up on top of the lid and screamed. "Help, the toilet is flooding!"

Chairs screeched across the floor above me and feet pounded down the stairs as my roommates stampeded over each other to come to the rescue.

What a bunch of morons they turned out to be. Instead of helping, they collapsed to the floor in hysterics.

I waved my arms above my head and shouted. "Ya'll can stop laughing now. Anyone happen to notice the *flood*?"

Finally, someone waded into the bathroom, reached behind me, lifted the lid to the tank, and jiggled a doohickey, which stopped the flow.

When they quit laughing enough to speak, one of them asked, "Why did you stand on the toilet and start screaming? Don't they have toilet plungers in Canada?"

"Ha ha. Someone obviously waltzed off with it, so I had to do something to keep the water in. Where I come from, when you put a lid on something, the stuff stays inside. This stupid lid is defective."

I was the butt of many jokes that year, but no one was smart enough to tell me the one thing I wanted to know. How are you supposed to know what you don't know if you don't know that you don't know it?

OUT WITH THE TIDE

IN MY DAY, which according to my son Garret was back when the Dead Sea was just getting sick, surveys in women's magazines touted the Laundromat as one of the hot spots to troll for a man.

For the record, locking eyes with a guy across the room who is sorting through his dirty underwear does not smack of romance.

It was definitely dirty laundry, not love, that took my cousin Sharon and I into the Laundromat one beautiful summer day.

I threw my clothes on the counter and started to sort. I had no qualms about the world eyeballing my soiled clothes if they had nothing better to do.

Sharon, however, was a different species. You would have thought she was making a secret deposit at Fort Knox. Everything was already sorted and in cloth sacks. Her underwear bag even had a combination lock on it. No one was going to sneak a peek at her granny pants.

We shared the three front-loading washing machines closest to the door. I nonchalantly put some clothes in each one, but Sharon looked both directions and then over her shoulder before she thrust hers in.

She reminded me of a criminal in a bad movie who cases the joint

before she rips something off the shelves. She was about as discreet as flashing lights on a police car.

One day when she was stuffing her dirty clothes into the washing machine, her bra caught on the button of her jacket. Her face turned purple with humiliation as she twisted and turned and hopped on one foot trying to hide the offending thing. It got so tangled, she finally shoved it up her sleeve and then stuck her head into the washing machine, pretending to be busy until people quit staring. I fell over laughing and shouted, "Encore!"

When she finally got her clothes stashed and started the wash cycle, we sat down across the room to relax and enjoy the warm breeze that blew through the open door. We chatted and thumbed through old copies of *Woman's Day* and *Reader's Digest*.

Suddenly, in the middle of the cycle, the door to the first machine exploded open. We jerked our heads up to see our clothes shoot out of the washer in a tidal wave of water and suds.

We stared at each other, stunned. There's nothing like a little conversation in the middle of a crisis. "Did you put too much soap in?" I asked.

"I don't think . . ." Suddenly she realized our underwear was surging out the door.

It was like fireworks on the Fourth of July. She shot off the chair and into the street. I was right there with her. It's not like we could ignore the situation.

Sharon, in her panic, slipped on the wet cement and smacked down on her bottom. People walking up the street tried to jump out of the way as she scrambled up. Some pressed themselves along the windows and walls of the Dineaway Restaurant next door to avoid our plundering.

They acted as if they had never seen two girls slosh through soapsuds gathering up underwear while it flowed down Main Street before. Did these people not watch TV? On second thought, with the two of us around, why would they need to?

We were both laughing—Sharon because she was in hysterics, me because I knew what my cousin would do when she got home and realized that the world had seen the red underwear that was showing under her wet white pants. Thank heavens my only clean pants that day were blue jeans.

When Rick and I met years later and began to talk about getting married, people warned him about my exploits, but he thought my disasters were funny. I quickly learned that marriage does strange things to a man's sense of humor.

All Locked Up

How is it possible that we live in an age of electronic and mechanical wonders like satellites in space, Google, and the iPhone, yet we still have people who have no workable lock on their bathroom door?

Perhaps these people do not understand that even though the doorknob came with the house, when it breaks, it can be replaced. It's not like it's made out of gold and you can only afford one in a lifetime and have to pass it down through all generations of time.

I know people who are meticulous about locking their front doors but seem to be blasé about a working lock for the bathroom. I am here to proclaim, I do not have a problem if someone walks into my house without an invitation, but I have a huge problem, call it a phobia, when someone walks in on me in the bathroom unannounced.

One of life's little luxuries should be to walk confidently into the water closet, lock the door, ensconce yourself on the throne as you pick up a good magazine, and enjoy a few stress-free moments.

Homeowners with no locks on the door should, at the very least, be considerate enough to have a dresser sitting in the room that you can move in front of the door to offer some sort of security.

Maybe they have no problem giving a shout-out as someone walks by, but personally, I don't like to advertise everything I am doing.

There is, however, another train of thought. Perhaps no lock on the bathroom door is part of a grand scheme to keep certain people from visiting. I can see the family emergency plan when some undesirable comes to visit.

"Stations everyone, Rick and Jane and their six kids are about to descend. Get the broken doorknob and screw it on the bathroom door."

That would certainly keep me from visiting. If I have to use the toilet plunger to hold the door to the bathroom shut, either I will never come again or my visit will be short and bathroom free. Come to think of it, I have some people I want to try this theory on.

It wasn't until I started to have children that I realized one thing worse than a bathroom with no lock on the door was a bathroom *with* a lock on the door.

One day, when Jason was not quite two, he locked himself in the bathroom. I panicked as I pictured rolls of toilet paper plugging the toilet and flooding the house. What if he filled the tub and then fell in and drowned? Maybe he'd get under the sink and eat the Comet. I could see my Mother of the Year award going down the drain—unless he clogged that too.

I closed one eye and peeked into the keyhole. "Jason, stay away from the toilet. Come to the door sweetheart." Silence!

I lay on my stomach and tried to look under the crack at the bottom of the door. Nothing. I stuck my finger through and wiggled. "Jason, come grab Mommy's finger."

That was brilliant. What good would that do? It's not like I was going to pull him out under the crack in the door.

"Stay there, son." Another brilliant statement. Where else would he go? "I'll be right back."

I rummaged through the junk drawer in the kitchen but couldn't find the key. I grabbed a bobby pin.

How did they do this in the movies? I rammed it into the keyhole and jiggled. I pulled it out, bent one of the prongs, and tried again. The stupid thing got jammed. I kept calling to Jason. He started laughing. Was that a sign of trouble?

I eyed the hinges. Maybe I could hammer them out and lift the door down. Where did Rick hide his tools? I didn't dare leave Jason to go find them. The door looked too heavy anyway. I would probably drop it and knock myself out cold.

We were living in Iowa at the time, where Rick was going to school. As much as I hated to do it, the only way out of this problem was to call him. I grabbed the phone book and sat down outside the bathroom door to listen for Jason.

Where the heck was the number? I thought you could find everything in the yellow pages. Was I supposed to look under *Palmer* or *Chiropractic*? Maybe it was listed under the Federal Government. Did they even have a published number? Finally I found it under *Colleges* and dialed the administration office.

Meanwhile Jason was banging something around. It sounded like the plunger. Great, there was a sanitary toy. I ran to the phone hanging in the kitchen and dialed.

"I need to talk to Rick Still. It's an emergency."

The cord on my phone wasn't long enough to reach the bathroom, so I walked as far as it would stretch and shouted. "Jason, what are you doing in there?"

"No, I don't know what his schedule is." I said to the operator when she asked me what class he was in. "Don't you have a record of it somewhere?"

She put me on hold! My son was locked in the bathroom and this . . . person on the other end of the line had me in some limbo land. She was no 911 operator.

A loud click brought me back to the planet. "We'll send a runner for him, ma'am."

"Tell them to hurry!"

I hung up, rushed back to the bathroom, and pasted my ear to the door.

I didn't hear any water running. Was that a good sign? "Jason, come to the door and talk to Mommy." I tried to get his attention with a rendition of his favorite song.

"The eensy weensy spider went up the water spout."

Oops! That song had water in it; better not give him any ideas.

"Jason, come to the door and play patty-cake with mommy."

I was getting nervous and started to beat the rhythm into the door. He started pounding back on the other side. At least I knew he was conscious.

A few minutes later, the phone rang. I dashed to grab it. It was my husband.

"Honey, why didn't you write down the phone number to the school? How come you never told me your schedule? You never tell me anything. What if someone died and I couldn't get ahold of you?"

"I thought you had an emergency," he interrupted.

"I do, and I had no idea where to tell them to find you."

"Jane, stop yammering and tell me what's wrong."

"Jason locked himself in the bathroom."

"Well, get him out."

"Gee, why didn't I think of that? I can't find the key, so I rammed a bobby pin into the lock, and now it's stuck. I was going to try to take the door off the hinges, but it's too big. You have to come home and do it for me. Hurry, he's been in there a long time."

"What's he doing?"

I rolled my eyes. "He's decorating a cake. Do I have X-ray vision?"

"Is he crying?"

"No he's not crying, I think he's playing with the toilet plunger."

"Did you ask him to unlock the door?"

"Of course I didn't ask him to unlock the door. He won't know how to do that. Will you please come home and take the door down?"

"Janie, just try it. If he is old enough to lock it, he can unlock it."

"That's ridiculous. He won't even understand me."

"Jane," irritation tinged his tone.

"All right, I'll ask, but it won't work." I put the phone down and walked back to the bathroom.

"Jason, will you unlock the door for Mommy, please?"

A moment later, the doorknob jiggled and the door opened. *I am an idiot!* He walked out, completely unharmed. Of all the moments in time, he had to pick this particular one to be obedient. I walked back to the phone.

"OK, so he's out." I choked on the words. "How does it feel to be right for a change?"

I heard a snort before the phone clicked off. When Rick got home, he gave me a copy of his class schedule, a lecture about only calling him at school for real emergencies, and then a hug. All I could say was "Honey, if you wanted someone who responded well to emergencies, you should have married an ambulance driver."

Losing the Children

My children's early years happened in the '80s, when the only thing scarier than fashion and big hair was the potential of being abducted by a stranger. Rick and I drilled safety measures into our children. We had our secret password, which they all remember to this day.

The one thing we neglected to discuss with them, however, was that the threat of being abducted by a stranger was not nearly so great a threat as being abandoned by their own flesh-and-blood mother.

It's not that I meant to abandon them—OK, so I had my moments, but I really didn't do it on purpose.

There was no excuse the first time. And it's not like we abandoned Jason. It's more like he ran off. Besides, he was my first child, and I was a novice. But when you have one toddler between four adults, and two of those adults are the grandparents, you're not the only one to blame.

We were shopping at the mall one day when I suddenly discovered Jason was missing. He had just turned two and had finally grown out of the huge frog-eye stage he had when he was a baby and was starting to get cute. Someone must have grabbed him, for sure.

I panicked and started to thrash through the round clothing racks calling his name. Grandma was gazing around the store, a little too calm for my liking, so I pushed her and Grandpa out of my way and told them to stay in the store and look while Rick and I ran into the mall.

We looked both ways and were about to split up when we noticed a sizeable crowd gathered in front of the wishing fountain. Great, Jason had drowned!

We elbowed our way to the front. Jason was entertaining the crowd by splashing and kicking around in the fountain, stark naked. Turns out that my scorn for women who couldn't keep their children from running outside naked had come back to slap me in the face.

How was I going to get him out of there without people knowing he was my offspring?

Rick was about to call out to him, but I stomped on his foot, glared at him, and headed for Jason.

"Little boy," I called, "you should come out of there. Your parents must be worried about you. Let me help you get dressed and find your mommy."

Jason stopped running for a moment, looked at me, and shouted, "Mommy, fun!"

Hundreds of eyes turned to stare at me. *Crap, now what should I do?* I did the first thing that came to mind. I jerked my head to the side and looked over each shoulder as if to see if his mother was behind me.

"Mommy, look."

By then my in-laws were attracted to the scene and my mother-in-law was beside me.

"Jane, aren't you going to get him?" she asked.

My face turned sixteen shades of red. Everybody started to laugh, including Rick—the traitor.

"Jason, come to Grandma." The woman had no pride.

I noticed a security guard coming to investigate, so I turned to Rick and told him to hurry and grab Jason. He ditched his shoes, rolled up his pants, and waded in.

Jason ran away screaming, "No, no, no!"

"Sir," the security guard called out, "you are not allowed to wade in the pond."

This was ridiculous. I had to laugh as Rick scooped up a slippery, wet Jason and hauled him, kicking and squealing, out of the water.

I grabbed Jason's clothes by the edge of the fountain and dressed him. Grandma dug around in her purse for some candy to quiet his protests. Rick and Grandpa dealt with the security guard.

"Sir, was there a reason you let your son go swimming in the water with no clothes on? Did he, uh, pee in there?"

Grandpa decided to get in on the act. "I told you it wasn't a good idea, son. Very unsanitary."

Rick didn't miss a beat, "Well, there were no signs posted. And no, he didn't pee in the water. He's a child prodigy. He potty trained early."

"The security guard narrowed his eyes as if to size Rick up. "This is highly irregular—indecent exposure and all."

I couldn't believe what I was hearing. I looked at the man, but I couldn't tell if he was serious.

"I'll let you off with a warning this time," he said. "Just don't let anything like this happen again. You're certain he didn't let his water go in the fountain?"

"Cross his heart." Grandpa felt compelled to get back in on the action.

The man gave us another once over and then shook his head, hitched up his pants, and walked away.

"Why didn't you just tell them that he ran away and climbed into the pool?" I asked.

"You wouldn't want Ricky to allow you to get arrested for your negligence, now, would you dear?" said my mother-in-law, jumping right in to defend her precious son.

"Oh, no." I smirked. "I'd far rather let people think my husband is an idiot."

One Brick Short of a Load

My Dad Liked to Say he was so tough that when he didn't have a razor he just rubbed his whiskers to the inside of his cheek and then bit them off.

Both of my brothers were provincial wrestling champions and liked to think they were tough guys too. All that muscle came in handy on moving day.

When my brothers helped Rick and I load up to move to California, I realized the literal act of airing my dirty laundry in public was only a prelude to my wash day blues.

Things were going well until it came time to load my washer. When Mark and Joe tried to heft the machine, they grunted.

"Janie, what have you got in here, bricks?"

"What a bunch of wimps you guys are. I just threw in some towels to make use of the empty space."

As they carried it to the truck, beads of sweat ran down their foreheads and the veins in their arms popped out and snaked across their biceps. I laughed at them and skipped off to grab another box. A moment later, I heard a shout.

"Janie, get the heck over here. NOW!"

It sounded like someone had popped a blood vessel. I dropped everything and ran. They stood beside the washing machine, holding the lid up.

"You almost killed us, Einstein."

I peeked inside. It was full to the top with soaking wet bath towels. I gave them a cheesy grin. "Oops."

I am the only one in my family with a sense of humor.

Some things in life come in threes. Unfortunately, it's never winning the lottery.

My third washing machine fiasco happened when we lived in Iowa, shortly after Jason locked himself in the bathroom.

It was a bright sunny day, and I was absorbed in the role of laundry diva. I played scratch and sniff with bibs, sleepers, and dirty shirts and grunted out words that will never appear in Webster's Dictionary.

I had just put away my "Hints from Heloise" stain removal guide when water started gushing out of the washing machine and onto the floor.

I stood there staring, my mouth open. It took a few moments for reality to hit before I did what any laundry diva would do. I shut my mouth and turned the cycle off. The water kept surging out. I thought for a moment and then reached behind and unplugged the washer. Nothing happened.

This definitely qualified as an emergency.

I charged to the phone and dialed the school. I wish I had thought to disguise my voice, but then, how many women would be calling the school every few days in crisis mode to ask for Rick?

"Yes, I have his schedule." I said into the mouthpiece.

"What class is he in now?" The efficient voice on the other end asked.

Don't these people ever run out of questions?

"Well, I don't know where it is right this second. The schedule is probably swirling around in the whirlpool I'm standing in."

The school sent runners out to track Rick down. He arrived breathless to the phone.

"Is this an emergency?"

"Of course it's an emergency. The washer won't shut off and water is pouring all over the floor."

"Did you turn it off?"

"Of course. Do you think I'm stupid?"

"I'm on my way home."

I needed scuba gear, but all I had was towels. I threw every one we owned onto the water gushing over the floor. I'd started using the clothes by the time Rick got home.

He pulled up his pant legs and slogged to the washer. "Janie, I thought you said you turned the water off."

"Hello. It's unplugged isn't it?"

He slapped his forehead and stared at me. "Honey, see these taps back here? You shut them off and the water will stop running."

Rick grabbed the broom and began sweeping water out the door. I gathered up the wet towels and carried them outside to wring them out on the lawn. "Where do they teach these things?" I shouted.

Rick started to laugh. I shook my head.

"Boy, is my shorthand coming in handy now."

visiting the sick and inflicted

when i am in the hospital, there is only one person I want to see, and that would be my husband. And he better be there to experience my pain and suffering and to anticipate my every need.

I do not want to see my children. They only come to steal my food, surf my channels, and zing my bed around like a carnival ride so they can see me puke into the cute turquoise dish designed for that express purpose. Besides, a break from the kids is one of the only benefits of being in the hospital.

I do not want to see my perky friends. They feel the need to come all dressed up in their cutest clothes with hair combed and makeup on.

If you feel you must visit me, please roll out of bed and come in your pajamas with mascara smeared under your eyes, morning breath, and bed hair. That might actually cheer me up. One look at you, and I would feel a whole lot better about myself. Instead of thinking about how horrible I felt, I would enjoy thinking about how bad you look.

I want armed guards—with pistols loaded—outside my door. It should be a service offered to everyone. You should not have to be rich and famous or a gangster to receive those privileges. No one would dare walk off the street into the president's or Lady Gaga's room.

Once, right after the birth of my son Adam, I had just dragged myself out of bed and into the bathroom after being up all night. Of course, I was sporting the beautiful, flowing designer gown the hospital provided, and I had added my own improvements in the form of blood, sweat, and a few tears.

The right side of my hair was smashed from sleeping on it, and the left side poked out like two porcupines attacking each other. Two-day-old black mascara was caked under my eyes, and it looked like they were attacked by a drunken tattoo artist.

After I flushed the toilet, which sounded like a Boeing 747 at take off, I yanked the door open and locked eyes with two young male missionaries sitting beside my bed.

I had once seen models stand outside of a store frozen like statues, and I had always wanted to try it. Apparently, that golden moment had arrived. I froze midstumble; my eyes bugged out in horror.

They jerked up off their chairs and shot out of the room. I don't think I will ever recover from the scars of that moment. I cursed them. First with a life of celibacy and then I recanted and wished upon each of them a wife, fatter and uglier than I was at that moment.

I could only hope they would not bring my name up in the next meeting at church, or I might have to shoot them.

I have been in that kind of meeting many times before, when the conversation centered on an afflicted member. One particular conversation is etched into my brain.

"Frank is doing much better since his hemorrhoid operation. As soon as his bowels move, he can go home."

Someone else piped up. "I remember when my friend Joe had hemorrhoids. He couldn't walk without writhing in pain. They were as big as giant marbles."

I was embarrassed for Frank and disgusted to discover that a segment of society actually discussed these things openly and with apparent pride. Later that day, the telephone tree called around to inform us that Frank was resting quietly at home. Everyone in the world knew his great accomplishment for the day. Should I send balloons?

While my circle of friends does not include Olympic athletes with gold medals or world-class bowling champions, I've had the good fortune of knowing people with kidney stones and gallstones that looked like the heads of shrunken pigmies. These people love to tote their prizes, stuffed in canning jars, to any hospital where I've had the misfortune of being incarcerated.

The only drawback, as far as I can see, to not having people come for hospital visits is the nurses will think you don't have any friends. Not that you care what the nurses think, but it could affect their behavior toward you.

If you are sweet and kind, they will treat you well. However, if you're cranky, they have all night to plot their revenge. After all, if no one else likes you well enough to visit, who will care?

My dad told me the nurses keep needles as big and dull as baseball bats and enemas in the freezer for people they don't like. That would explain why he hates hospitals.

It's not that I don't want people to think of me. I like flowers and chocolate, balloons and chocolate, cards and chocolate, and books and chocolate.

Why can't people just send their gifts or drop them off at the front desk without feeling obligated to stay? That would solve the problem of the nurses thinking you have no friends.

Hallmark should have a set of special invitation cards with instructions for the few people you would actually like to see. The best time to visit would be the middle of the night, since that is when the nurses come and wake you up to see if you are sleeping.

My card would say, "You are cordially invited to the sickbed of Jane Still at St. John's Hospital on the sixth floor. She is accepting visitors only between the hours of two and four a.m. Ugly yourself up and bring chocolate."

DOCTOR BLUES

THERE IS ONLY ONE THING WORSE than a hysterical woman; that is a hysterical man. It's especially annoying when that man is your husband.

Our first baby was only home from the hospital one week when I witnessed the transformation of my six-foot, 180-pound, provincial-wrestling-champion-of-his-weight-class-in-high-school husband change into a clucking, fussing, old biddy hen. His conversations centered on Jason's health and well-being.

"Janie, remember Jason's head is like a blob of Jell-O. You have to support his neck when you hold him."

"Thanks for reminding me, hon. Don't worry, if he gets too jiggly I'll just throw him in the freezer to firm him up a bit."

"Honey, Jason's welfare is not a laughing matter."

Rick had developed a baby ritual. It reminded me of the kind of thing a man does when he goes to buy a new car. Each time he picked Jason up, he went through what I like to call his "kicking the tires routine."

First, there was the sniff test. He would bend over to sniff the diaper and then call for a second opinion.

"Jane, does his diaper need changing?"

"I just changed him, but you can check." I knew he would. He'd unsnap Jason's sleepers, lift his leg, and peek inside the diaper. Then if it was safe, he'd run his fingers inside for reassurance.

The day his finger test coincided with one of Jason's special deliveries would be the day he quit checking.

"Honey, don't you think these sleepers are too tight? They seem to be choking him."

I rolled my eyes. "I gave him mouth to mouth once already today. Is he turning blue again?"

I knew what was coming next, so I walked into the living room with a Q-tip and the bottle of hydrogen peroxide. Rick had unsnapped the offending pajamas and was inspecting his belly button.

"How many times did you clean this today? It looks infected to me."

"I filled the tub up with hydrogen peroxide this morning and spent the day splashing around with him."

I suppose I should be grateful he was so conscientious. I just wished his perfectionism extended to doing the dishes and picking his socks off the lamp when he kicked them off every night.

After Jason was checked out and aired out and I was stressed out, Rick redressed him, swaddled him in blankets, and then set him on his knees to stare at him. It reminded me of the way I looked at a piece of meat while I figured out how to cook it.

"Jane, come feel Jason. He's hot."

"He has fourteen blankets on him, take one off."

"Then he'll be cold. I think he's sick. You need to take him to the doctor."

"I have been there three times this week already. I refuse to be your surrogate hypochondriac. Do you know how it feels to have everyone in the clinic give me the oh-there's-that-poor-hysterical-new-mother look again?"

"I still think you should . . ."

I stood my ground. "I took him yesterday because you thought he was throwing up more than he ate, two days ago because you said he had a rash, and Monday it was because he didn't poop often enough to suit you. Now you think he's too hot? If you want to make a fool of yourself, you take him."

Of course, he wouldn't. Apparently, that fell under my job description. After all, I had been going there for so many months, Rick thought it should feel as natural as going to the bathroom by now.

Wrong! If I had a choice of going to the doctor or plucking the hair inside my nose, I'd pick plucking every time.

Maybe I should meet Rick at the door every evening, dressed in a white coat and brandishing a butcher knife while I chased him down for a little sample of his blood. He'd learn familiarity did not always breed comfort. I would get a little exercise, a new coat, and a husband with a new attitude.

The picture made me laugh until I imagined myself slipping and ending up in the hospital, cranky, with a nurse bending over me prepping a frozen enema.

Fashion Faux Pas

I hated going to the doctor's office for many reasons, but my main concern centered on clothing—I worried about what to wear.

When I grew up I had one outfit for church. Every week I wore my Sunday dress, socks, and shoes. On school days, I wore my school clothes. After school, I changed into play clothes.

Now that I was acquainted with the protocol required for prenatal care and the rigmarole of all the check-ins, checkups, and check-overs, I needed a 'going to the doctor' wardrobe. I wanted outfits with no complicated fasteners, zippers, or buttons in the back or a tight neck. It had to be something that wouldn't wreck my hair and I could whip off in a frenzy.

When I was in college, I was on the ballroom dance team and went to Europe. I won the quick-change award. Little did I know how handy that skill would be in my childbearing years.

I was paranoid about not being dressed when the doctor came into the room. If I wasn't as fast as Superman in the telephone booth, the doctor might walk in and discover me in my undies.

It could happen, I knew. I had worked in physical therapy in my premarriage years and walked in on a patient once.

I was so shocked by the incident that instead of simply closing the door, I stood and engaged him in conversation.

"Oh! I am so sorry. I thought you would be dressed by now."

His pants were around his ankles and his arms were flailing around in an effort to cover himself.

"My back is killing me or I would be."

"Can I help you?"

"I can manage. I'd just like a little privacy."

He half hopped over and grabbed the back of a chair to keep from tipping over, his pants twisted around his ankles.

"I could take your pants off." I took a step into the room.

His face turned red. Did I really just tell him I would take his pants off?

"Uh, just crack the door when you're done."

His eyes looked a little crazed, but he nodded as I backed out and closed the door. When I turned to walk away, I was jerked back. My jacket had caught in the door, and I was stuck with my nose pressed into the wood.

Great, now when he came to open the door I'd fall on top of him. If I opened the door again, it would look like I was trying to sneak another peek. What if he could see my coat poking out on the other side of the door? He'd know I was standing there like an idiot.

I had to get it out. I slowly turned the knob and pushed the door open just enough to slide my coat out.

A chair crashed, and I heard a panicked, "I'm not dressed yet."

"No hurry. My coat was caught in the door. Take all the time you need. I'm not trying to rush you."

Shut up already, Jane! I said under my breath. I pulled my coat out and shut the door. The man was probably a cripple now.

"Please Lord, could you just take me now?" That was the moment I became permanently scarred.

The pregnancy doctor wasn't my only problem. I felt just as inept with the nurse. It seemed that no matter what the exam was, it required some level of undress. I could never be sure how much nakedness the nurse required. I certainly didn't want to look like an imbecile by asking her to clarify exactly what "take off all your clothes" meant.

Did she mean *all my clothes*, or did she just mean the clothes pertinent to the exam? Why should I take off my jeans if I was having my lungs looked at? It would be embarrassing to take off more than I needed to. That would make me look eager.

If I must remove all my clothes, what about my socks? A person needed something on for warmth and security, but socks look dorky when you're naked, and who wants to look like a dork?

Maybe, if I wore the right style and color, they would coordinate with the gown. Would knee socks look better or rolled ankle socks? Maybe socks that slid over my feet and didn't hit the ankle would be best.

Would black socks look better than white? Maybe they would let me take a gown home and try it on in the mirror.

What if you had a hole in your sock? It would look stupid to put your shoes back on to hide it, like you were ready to leap up after the exam and wear your gown the rest of the day as you ran your other errands.

I used to be frustrated with people who used the excuse, "I'm sorry I won't be able to make that commitment today. I'm going to the doctor."

Now I understood what they meant. They were having a panic attack. Not about what the doctor might do to them but about what they were going to wear. By the time the doctor got to you, you were numb, exhausted, and ready to comply with every indignity.

As I look back, I realize these problems would all disappear if the fashion world simply addressed this fashion faux pas in the doctor's office. It is the only place in the universe where no matter how rich or poor, famous or anonymous you are, it is a one-size-fits-all world.

Hmmm . . . bling gowns. I feel opportunity knocking.

Broken records

in case no one noticed, I am not the *Encyclopedia Britannica.* Nor do I get paid to keep medical records. The hospital has someone on staff to do just that. So why is it when you go to the clinic they ask you the same questions over and over?

Someone is obviously not doing their job. Perhaps they were under the misconception that if they asked me the same questions often enough, I would get the hint that I was supposed to care.

Apparently, a "good mother" has certain events carved in her memory that she could flip through like a rolodex.

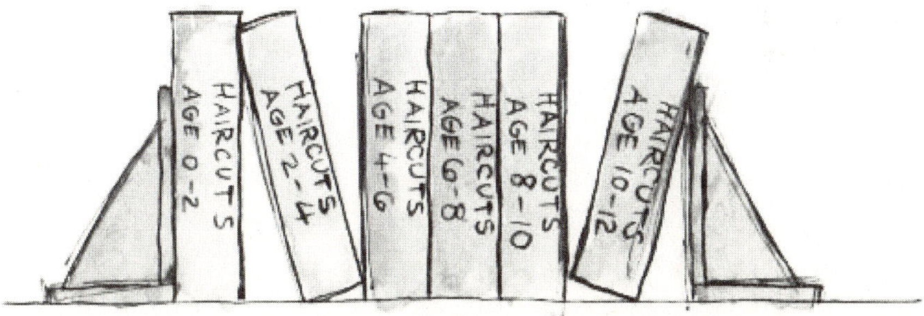

"Exactly when did little Johnny sit up, roll over, crawl, stand, walk, and bark?" The receptionist sat with pencil poised. "Spit it out—the exact hour would be perfect. Month and day will do."

They required the date of each child's first tooth and first molar, the name and birth date of each sibling, plus shoe size. When did they start eating solids? Blah, blah, blah, blah, blah. The only question they left unasked was the number of eyelashes and the length in centimeters—something I would actually be curious about.

I longed to smile and tell them I knew the exact second that each of these momentous events occurred. I had nothing better to do each day than to lie on my stomach and gaze, starry eyed, at each precious moment of my baby's life with pen in hand, so I could mark these historic events in the annals of time.

The only question I managed to answer correctly was the exact day they started sleeping through the night.

Did I mention that every visit I made, they asked me the same questions? Like I was going to suddenly remember this year what I couldn't remember last year.

I was not the type of mother to throw a coming out party when my children rolled over or sat up for the first time. I celebrated milestones in my own simple way.

"Listen up everyone, Briana has her first tooth. If you value your fingers, keep them out of her mouth."

"Hey, Garret is crawling now, keep him away from the . . . oops. Someone haul him back up the stairs."

"Hallelujah, let's have a party. I think Kristjana is going to be potty trained before she goes to college after all."

Why did people need this information, anyway? I was not the least bit interested what day I first sat up. It was my educated guess that each of my children would sit and roll over before they entered first grade and be fully potty trained before they went to university.

On a good day, I did remember my children's names. If I didn't get them in the right order, I could at least say them all. On a bad day I really only had to remember my boys' names, Jason, Adam, and Garret. My girls, Ariana, Kristjana, and Briana would answer to Ana 1, Ana 2, Ana 3. I sounded like Lawrence Welk tapping his toe and waving his baton before striking up the band.

How was I supposed to remember whose birthday was on the fifth one month and whose was the sixth the next when I forgot my own birthday?

I'm still not clear in what year I was married. I have to remember how old Jason is and count backwards. It is simply too hard to do the math. Besides, shouldn't they have a record of these things that follows each child?

By the time the brain gymnastics were over, I was ready to lie out on a stretcher in the morgue and eat a bucket of chocolate.

I had good intentions of keeping track of milestones, but somehow my first inclination to their "firsts" was not to dig around through drawers to find the dang baby book.

I did try to mark some of the events on calendars, but it never got into their books. I kept the calendars, but they are stashed somewhere and will likely reappear only when I'm dead. That is the moment my children will appreciate the fact that I was not my friend Tracy, who happens to be every statistician's dream.

She has a baby book for each year of her children's lives plus another smaller one for major events like their first owie, every bath they ever took, and their first haircut, which includes a photo and journal entry of each hair's journey through life.

My children will rejoice that they will not have to fill a U-Haul trailer with so many books that they'll have to build a special wing onto their home for exhibition.

That is the day I will be exonerated.

Hairy Scary

IF I WALKED OUT of a beauty salon with my hair standing on top of my head in spikes dyed orange, purple, and red, I might want to call the bomb squad to take care of a certain beauty establishment. But, for some people, it was their signature statement.

In the '80s, the statement women were making was a spiral perm, and I had to have one.

There was one insurmountable barrier, a measly fifty-dollar bill. So what if we were poor college students and that represented our entire food budget for two weeks? I was willing to starve for my vanity, and Rick could feast on my beauty. I dug out my weapons and prepared my assault.

"Not tonight, honey. I have to sleep with my head in this position or my curlers will hurt and give me a headache."

Rick started to laugh. "Who ever heard of saying no because of an anticipated headache?"

"You try sleeping with sharp thingies jabbing you in the head all night.

"Why can't you use your curling iron?"

"I have to take care of Jason. I don't have time to spend hours of the day curling my hair."

Rick sat up. "Why don't you wear your curlers during the day then?"

"Honey, you don't expect me to run around in public looking like someone from outer space, do you?"

"That's better than having our sex life ruled by your hair!"

"Honey, what do you want me to do, get a spiral perm? We can't afford that."

"Jane, I like your hair the way it is."

I like to think it says a lot for my natural wit and charm that before we were married I even came across Rick's radar screen. He had a ridiculous rule about dating anyone with short hair. He never broke that rule until he met me.

Over the years, he asked me to grow my hair out, and I was glad I had. However, I discovered that marriage brought out my criminal tendencies when it came to getting my way about something I really wanted, and I was about to engage in round two of my scheme.

"Hon, maybe it's just better if I cut my hair. It would be so much easier to take care of. You're right, as usual. It's not fair to you for me to wear curlers to bed."

"I thought you liked your hair long."

"I do, but a woman has to sacrifice for her family sometimes. A spiral perm costs fifty dollars, and since we don't have that much money and you don't want me to wear curlers to bed, I should just cut it. Besides, I look good in short hair. I could even save us money and cut it myself."

Rick choked. "Yeah, like the time you trimmed my beard? By the time you were done it looked like a rat chewed my face."

"Well at least we would save ten dollars. A perm would cost us forty dollars more. Of course, by the time I paid for a few more haircuts it would be the same as a perm. With a perm, you don't have to worry about cutting your hair. You can let it grow."

"So Janie, why don't you just get a perm?"

"Honey, we can't afford it. We have to buy food."

"I'm sure we can manage. You'll think of something."

I smiled, as the ultimate idea just happened to occur to me.

"We could host a couple of potlucks and keep all the leftovers. My perm won't cost us a thing."

Rick began pulling the curlers from my head. Apparently, he had a little larceny in him too.

I practically skipped into the beauty salon two days later. There was only one hairdresser in the shop, and I introduced myself to the marvelous creature who was about to transform my boring coif into sensational curls. Her eyes squinted in my direction, and her mouth pinched in as she sized me up. She blew air out of her nose and said, "It is impossible to perm long hair. You'll have to get it cut first."

That should have been the first clue I wasn't going to walk out of there looking like Miss America. I tried to think of something to say that didn't indicate how stupid I thought her statement was.

"Lots of people with spiral perms have longer hair than mine." That was brilliant.

She walked over to me and ran her fingers through it as if she was combing through a horse's mane.

"It's awfully thick."

I didn't say a word and suppressed the desire to whinny and paw the ground.

"Well, all right," she said, "but we'll have to be careful."

Why didn't I have the sense to giddy up out of there? But no, I was bent on being the proud owner of prize-winning corkscrew curls.

"Now," she said after she had it all rolled, "it's very important that we take your hair out as soon as the timer rings. We don't want your hair to burn, do we?"

We most assuredly don't, I thought.

I thumbed through my magazine while the woman moved this jar and that and did a little cursory sweep of the floor. She continued her mindless chores until about five minutes before the timer was to ring.

"I'll just make a quick call. When the timer rings, we'll get those curlers right out."

When the bell buzzed, she walked across the room until the cord stretched to its breaking point and turned it off. She looked at me, smiled, held up one finger, and continued her conversation.

Are you kidding me? This conversation couldn't have been made at any time during the thirty-five minutes she was flicking dust off her fingernails?

"Uh, excuse me," I pointed to my hair after a couple of minutes passed. "Remember me? The lady whose hair is about to incinerate?" She ignored me.

I was in a bad movie where the airhead secretary was in a mindless conversation about her idiotic boyfriend. Another five minutes went by. I was sure I smelled smoke. Did Emily Post have a rule for a situation like this?

I gave her my freaked out face where my eyes get big, my lower lip drops, and my teeth grit. I jabbed my pointer fingers into the air on each side of my head.

She covered the mouthpiece and moved her lips.

"It will be fine. Don't worry."

I wasn't worried, I was schizophrenic. My hair was going to fry. I was going to be ripping bald. She abruptly ended the conversation when my eyes went wild and I started to tear the curlers out and throw them in her direction.

"Don't do that. We have to rinse it first." She breezed across the room to the sink and beckoned me to follow. "I do this everyday. Your hair will be perfect."

I needed to believe her, so I took a deep breath and leaned back into the sink. Maybe I had over-reacted; after all, my head wasn't in flames—yet.

The moment of unveiling arrived. She sat me in the chair in front of the mirror and removed the towel. Perfect, bouncy, spiral curls.

I looked at the clock. This had taken longer than I thought.

"My husband has an exam, and I need to get home to take care of the baby. How long will this take to dry?"

"The best thing to do is let it air dry. I'll trim it up, and you can leave. Be sure not to wash it for a couple of days."

I sailed out of the salon. I couldn't take my eyes from the rearview mirror. Dang, I was gorgeous.

Rick rushed out of the house as I walked through the door. He didn't even notice me.

I played with Jason until my hair was dry and then went to get dressed for an interior decorating class I had that evening. I walked past a mirror hanging over the couch, did a double take and screamed.

My hair was huge—no, it was ginormous! I tried to go into the bathroom to get another mirror, but my hair was so big it bounced off the door jam. I had to squeeze it in sideways.

I had a final in an hour, and I was pretty sure I'd have to unroll the windows for my head to fit into the car. I could try wetting it down again but if it dried before class was over, it would swallow up the people sitting next to me.

I needed one of those portable showers so I could keep pulling the string and soaking my head every few minutes. Like that would make people notice me less. I had to do something fast.

I pulled it into a ponytail, but I didn't have an elastic big enough so I twisted it into a bun. I looked like I had a Pomeranian sitting on top of my head. This was worse than any nightmare I'd ever had.

I grabbed the ponytail further up, pushed the rest of the hair down, twisted the upper half into a small bun on top of my head, and then attacked it with bobby pins.

My hair looked like Barbra Streisand in *Hello, Dolly!*, except on me it looked like a genie floating away in a turban made out of a down comforter. Gee, which glamorous "do" should I grace the world with?

I heard the front door close. Rick was home. Why didn't they build houses with secret passages anymore? There was no hiding my mess this time, so I tucked my feet under me and floated out to meet him.

Rick normally has squinty eyes, but for a moment they got so big I thought he'd had eye surgery. His hand flew to cover his mouth, and he spoke through his fingers. "Is that the look you were going for?"

"Yes, I thought I'd dye it orange now, join the circus, and put you through school. Don't you even think about laughing. My hair is ruined!"

Rick reached his hand out to touch it. "It looks like a helmet. You didn't pay for this, did you?

"I'll be getting my money back." I snapped and headed out the door for class.

Rick called after me. "At least you look good with your hair up."

You would think he had more pride than to let me go out in public.

I strode into class as if wearing a king-sized feather comforter wrapped around my head was the height of fashion on the Paris runway. I chose a seat in the back so my head wouldn't block anyone's view. Everyone gawked. I smirked with my lips, but my eyes dared them to say something.

My friend Rhonda tried not to laugh too hard and told me my hairstyle was called the "Gibson Girl." Most people could only achieve the look with rats or wads of cotton wrapped around their heads. Gee, wasn't I blessed!

The next day, I stormed the beauty parlor with my hair unleashed—a cross between Gene Wilder and Albert Einstein.

I grimaced at three clients sitting by the door. A bad hairdo is often a matter of opinion, but sometimes it's a matter of common consensus. They eyeballed me and started murmuring in low tones. Suddenly they all stood up and backed toward the door.

"Are you leaving because of my hair?" I called out to them.

They nodded.

"Don't walk, run. Run!" I pointed to the monster who was now taking money from her latest victim. "She did this to me. Hurry before she gets her hands on you too."

Wow! Who knew it was this much fun to clear a room?

I turned to face my nemesis, head up and shoulders squared. "I want my hair fixed and my money back."

She didn't even blink. "I warned you your hair was too long to perm. The best I can do for you is to give you some conditioners. We don't rcfund moncy hcrc."

"Conditioners! You offer me conditioner! I have been to four different salons this morning already for advice to fix my hair. I've got enough conditioners to float a boat." I handed her the receipts.

My hair is so fried I can't even get it cut. It would stick straight out of my head like a giant Chia pet hit by lightning. I am not walking out of here without a hundred dollars."

She stepped closer and leered down at me. I swear I could smell garlic on her breath.

"It's not my fault you chose to buy your hair products somewhere else."

I wanted to freshen her mouth with a baseball bat, but I am not a violent person.

"You are the last person I would go to for advice. Pay me or I am going to come and clear this room every day."

The manager picked that moment to walk out of his office. I jerked my head in his direction. His eyes widened in shock as my hair brushed two pictures hanging two feet away on the wall. I knew immediately that I was getting my money refunded. It was an unwritten understanding that I would never be back.

There was one valuable lesson in all this, however. I learned something I never knew before. How to French braid my own hair.

nightmare on elm street

WHEN I WAS GROWING UP, my greatest nightmare was showing up for school in my underwear. My arms would chop through my closet like propellers, whipping garments off the hangers until I was almost buried alive in discarded clothing I couldn't coordinate.

My panic choked me as the clock moved closer to the hour. Suddenly I was standing in front of my jeering class in bright polka-dot underpants while I tried to crunch myself into a ball. I always woke up out of breath and sweating.

I am sure this indicates some repressed part of my personality, but I prefer to think it is a healthy expression of my desire not to land myself in jail. If there were no laws, I might find nudity a thrifty alternative to shopping. Then what would I do for a phobia?

Once I had children, the nightmares revolving around my wardrobe malfunctions expanded. What does one wear to the emergency room or to a drowning or a kidnapping? Apparently nothing. In my nightmares, I always arrived naked.

I tried to talk to Rick about my fears, but in the early days of our marriage, he thought the art of communication was the name of a picture hanging in the Louvre.

"Honey, I'm just saying, maybe my nightmares about being naked in public are because we have no emergency plan. Wouldn't you sleep better at night if our kids knew how to get help in an emergency?"

"Janie, I have no problem sleeping at night. I don't have to arrive looking like a fashion plate everywhere I go."

I smirked at him. "I could always arrange for you to have problems sleeping, and the world is well aware you are not a fashion plate."

"Jane, the children are young. They don't worry about showing up to school in their underwear. In fact, they have no problem running through the streets naked. I don't think you should pass your fears on to them."

"I won't pass on my fears. I do not intend to raise a nudist colony. I will empower them."

"Jane, did you forget what happened to your friend Chantelle when she taught her kids to dial 911?"

Why is it that men can never remember things like taking out the garbage or mowing the lawn but they can be counted on to remember something you wish you never told them?

One day, when Chantelle was sick, the doorbell rang. She looked like a commercial for a vampire movie where the heroine had all the blood sucked out of her body. She staggered to the door, hair in snarls, nose red, and with a hacking cough.

She had a Zicam up her nose and was in midsnort as she pulled the door open to an imposing cut-the-small-talk police officer.

"Ma'am, are you taking drugs?" he asked.

"Are you a cop?" Even in the throes of death, nothing gets by Chantelle.

"Ma'am, are you taking drugs?" He stepped forward as she finished snorting.

"No, no they're medicinal drugs. I'm sick. What are you doing here?"

"You called 911."

"Do I look like I want to drag myself out of bed for visitors?"

"Ma'am, I can assure you this is not a social call."

Suddenly a ray of light penetrated through her foggy brain. "McKenna!"

Obviously when she taught her daughter how to call 911, she had not adequately defined the word *emergency*.

"You very sick, Mommy," her little girl said.

"You do look like you could use an ambulance, lady," said the police officer.

I don't care how bad she has let her appearance slip; no woman wants to hear that she looks like she needs an ambulance. Chantelle slammed the door and crawled back to bed.

"Honey," I continued, "Jason is nine years old, not three."

Rick rolled his eyes and shook his head while he gave me his broad, closed-mouth grin that brought out the dimple on his right cheek. I knew I had worn him down.

We gathered the kids together and made it clear that emergencies usually contained three important elements: blood, pain, and trauma.

One evening, shortly after our conversation, we decided to have a test run. We left Jason in charge and went to visit some neighbors down the street.

About twenty minutes later, Rick returned home. Instead of going into the house, he pulled the garbage cans onto the street for garbage

collection the next day. A few minutes later, a policecar, ambulance, and fire truck screamed up the street with sirens blaring and lights flashing.

"Boy, someone's in big trouble." Rick thought. To his horror, the vehicles screeched alongside our curb.

It would have been a cardiac arrest moment for me, but Rick kept a cool head. They leaped out of their vehicles and charged up to him. "What's the emergency?"

"No emergency here."

"Someone called."

"I think I'd know if I called you or not."

Suddenly Ariana threw open the door and yelled, "Jason's bleeding."

Everyone rushed into the house. The kids circled Jason, who was lying on the floor with a wad of toilet paper shoved between his teeth. He had decided to yank out his loose tooth. Blood had "shot out like a fountain," so he called 911.

"I'm sorry, officers." Rick apologized. "This whole thing is my wife's idea of compensating for her fear of showing up naked in public."

Apparently, that was too much information for our brave men in uniform, and they left. Probably to go straight home and address any fears their own wives harbored.

I wondered if now was a good time to tell Rick about the time Chantelle's babysitter called the police because she couldn't get the kids to bed. The police showed up the same time as Chantelle and Dan.

It might make him feel better to know that at least our kids weren't so bad the police had to bed them down for the night.

I didn't think Rick was ready for that little pearl just yet, but at that moment, I realized how much I loved Chantelle. She always makes me look good.

Drama Queen

"Unless you're dead, don't bother me when I am on the telephone!"

OK, maybe that language is a little extreme, but why do my children have all their little emergencies when I am trying to talk on the phone? It's like built-in sonar from their mouths to the phone line.

I would have suspected radar hiding in their noses or ears, but the doctor would have found it when he went in after all the beans and dry macaroni they had stuffed in their heads over the years.

My children have all day to get my attention, but it isn't until I am on the phone that catastrophes strike. Someone's bottom needs to be wiped, the toilet overflows, or other incessant complaints.

"Mo-o-m, Garret is looking at me. Make him stop."

"Mom, what are we having for breakfast tomorrow?"

"Can we come back in the house?"

"Adam said Rudolph the Red-Nosed Reindeer is dead!"

I tried to outsmart them by pretending to go to the bathroom, but suddenly it turned into a community watering hole. They didn't let something like a locked door stand in their way. Their determination to train me to stay off the phone was relentless.

If I had to make a call, I waited until the kids were playing happily outside or otherwise engaged before I tried to sneak away.

I would creep into the bedroom, lie on my stomach with my head under the bed, pick up the receiver, and muffle the touch-tone with a pillow. Just as I started a meaningful dialogue, peace would disintegrate and my bedroom would be overrun by the little terrorists.

My telephone conversations often went like this: "Hello, Tracy—"

"Don't walk in on your sister in the bathroom; she doesn't like it."

"I called about the meeting tomorrow—"

"I don't care if your brother was putting ice cream in your hair, you are not allowed to slug him."

"Amber doesn't know where I live and has no way to get here. Would you—"

"Put those scissors down. You may not cut the dog's eyelashes."

"Tracy, are you still there? What were we talking about? Oh yes, could you please—"

"Drop that knife. Now!"

I dropped the phone and left Tracy hanging while I chased after the delinquent.

It's no wonder, with all their trivial problems, that I learned to ignore them and continue my conversation. Unless there was an earthquake and the ceiling fell in or the toilet overflowed to the point you needed a lifeboat, I tuned it all out.

One day Kristjana was at the neighbors' showing off. "Look at me! I can hold my breath until my face gets bright red."

When she woke up after passing out, her chin was bleeding. She came bawling home.

"Mo-o-m!" I glanced at the tiny drop of blood on her chin and gave my typical response.

"Go put a cold washcloth on it. You'll be fine. Your dad will be home in a minute to look at it."

Rick came home about fifteen minutes later. Kristjana was still sitting on the steps, a bloody washcloth held up to her chin.

"Daddy, I cut my chin, and I'm pretty sure I'm going to die."

"Jane! Aren't you watching this child?"

The little drama queen; all she needed were three stitches.

Become One With the Water

Rick was not the one to be preaching to me about my bedside manner. His response to emergencies was, "drink more water."

"Daddy, my elbow hurts."

"Drink more water."

Briana came to him one day. "Dad, my knee hurts when I bend it."

"Don't bend it."

"Is that what you tell a patient when their back hurts—don't bend it?" she asked.

"Nope. Drink more water."

One day Kristjana managed to fracture her finger. She showed her Dad the bruise.

"You're not drinking enough water."

Garret got hurt once when he and Adam were wrestling. I loved to watch them. They looked like two bear cubs rolling and grunting around the floor.

"Dad, I think I hurt my shoulder."

Rick sat him down, palpated his shoulder, and gave him an adjustment. His parting words—"Drink some water."

Garret has a high pain tolerance, but every once in a while during the

next few days when he and Adam started goofing off, he would complain about his shoulder.

"Mo-om, my shoulder is so-o-o-re. Tell Dad to fi-i-i-x it."

"Your dad said you need to drink more water."

He had just started high school, and several days after his injury were wrestling tryouts. He made the team, but every day he came home from practice I heard him bellow through the house.

"Mo-om, my shoulder is so-o-o-re. Tell Dad to fi-i-i-x it."

"Rick, will you please take care of Garret's shoulder. He runs around here like a goat run through by a picador in a bullfight.

"Jane, it can't be that bad. He wrestles for heaven's sake. He's just a little sore. Give him more water."

"Honey, if I sat him in the ocean and he drank the stupid thing dry, he'd still be miserable."

"Of course he would. Do you have any idea what all that salt would do to him?"

"Stop it. I really think he's hurt."

Garret came upstairs. "Da-a-a-d, my shoulder hu-r-r-r-ts."

"Here's some water."

"Rick! I feel like the plumber's wife who always has leaky pipes. Why can't you just pretend he's a patient and take an X-ray?"

"Get your coat, son, or your mom's going to keep banging on her pipes."

I love, love, love being right. Garret had a broken collarbone, and I had something to lord over Rick. Life was good.

mothering instinks

I DON'T KNOW if I inflicted emotional trauma on my children when I raised them, but I have my own scars. If I could peel all my guilt away, I'd be at least three sizes smaller.

My children had plenty of issues with me. One was my housekeeping. They liked to compare me to the star of the popular '90s television show "Full House" where Danny Tanner walked around with a vacuum in one hand and waved a dust cloth in the other.

According to them, I was "Danny Tanner on crack." They thought it was ridiculous to vacuum the outside walls and under the eaves. They had a standing joke.

"We can't have anyone over to dinner tonight. Mom hasn't had time to go outside and dust the ivy." As if!

Surprisingly, they held no resentment or memory that I was—I can barely bring myself to say it—a tightfisted, hard-hearted, Band-Aid grinch.

In my defense, the little felons were constantly ripping off my Band-Aids.

Wrappers were strewn all over the house without so much as a drop of blood to show for the extravagance.

I don't know why, but it gave me warm fuzzy feelings to go to my cupboard and see boxes of bandages lined up nice and neat, ready for any emergency.

I felt the same about my canned fruits and vegetables, side by side in happy rows on my storage shelves. I had that same passion for the meat in my freezer. It's obvious I was one sick puppy, but I couldn't help myself. It was part of my heritage.

Once I saw my Aunt Marg pick up half a clothespin from the floor and put it in her pocket. "You never know when you will find the other half," she told me.

It had to be my grandmother's fault. She raised Aunt Marg, and when I went to live with her, she drilled it into me that the next big depression was around the corner. It's definitely her fault I was a Band-Aid hoarder.

On the other hand, it's also possible I developed my grinch tendency because I was afraid of raising a bunch of hypochondriacs. Every day at least one child stumbled, screaming through the house, and prostrated himself at my feet in the throes of death, screaming over an itty-bitty scratch.

They didn't even need to be hurt to want one. One day I caught Jason encouraging Garret to find where I hid the Band-Aids. Jason held onto Garret's legs while Garret stood on a stool that was balancing on a chair teetering on a step stool. Why couldn't they apply these same instincts to finding their shoes or coats?

Since raising a bunch of hypochondriacs or wasting good bandages on imaginary owies was out of the question, each wound had to be validated in triage.

Injuries that were invisible without a microscope were treated simply by ripping off the corner of a square of toilet paper. No sense in wasting toilet paper, not with the depression around the corner.

For a scratch that just broke the skin and had little or no blood, I splurged on one whole square. If there was blood, it would stick; if not, I wet it and slapped it on. When water wasn't handy, spit was extremely medicinal.

My grandmother and aunt would have been proud of my thrifty ways. After all, money did not grow on trees. Did I mention I had that depression to worry about, let alone our retirement fund to consider? I must have saved at least thirty dollars over the years; too bad I never invested it. Imagine the millions it would be making me now.

I was heartless. Why didn't I just snuggle my kiddies up and plaster them with bandages? My children felt every little bump and imaginary scrape as acutely as an amputation until it made contact with a Band-Aid. Nothing was quicker in stopping a sniffle and wringing a smile.

The day Jason came home from school with a Band-Aid plastered across his mouth was the day that I knew my mothering instincts were akin to Attila the Hun's.

He walked through the door, his eyes sparkling with pride. I stared. *What on earth . . . ?* He didn't appear hurt. Maybe he was so naughty in school the teacher had stuck a Band-Aid on his mouth to shut him up!

"Jason, what happened?"

A sword pierced my heart when both hands flew to protect his Band-Aid from the grinch.

"Were you talking in class?"

He shook his head.

"Did you hurt your mouth?"

He nodded.

"Can I look at it?"

I watched his eyes as he weighed the question.

"I won't take it off." I reassured him.

He held one finger up to keep me at bay and slowly pulled the Band-Aid away from the corner of his mouth.

I leaned over to peek. There was absolutely no sign of blood or a mark.

"I bit my lip, so my teacher gave me a Band-Aid."

He promptly pasted it back in place and went to flaunt the badge of courage to his brothers and sisters.

My heart dropped like an anchor. His teacher loved him more than I did. Then it hit me. It didn't come out of her pocket. The school board paid for that Band-Aid. They could afford it. I paid my taxes.

I went back to my penny-pinching habits. I deserved to suffer. I wonder if a Band-Aid would take away the owie on my heart.

Florence Nightingfail

Most of the little scratches the children cried about could be taken care of with a piece of toilet paper or a Band-Aid, but once in a while my scrapbooking instincts kicked in and my first choice in an emergency was a camera.

One day Kristjana and Briana went for a bike ride with two friends, Amber and KC. Thank goodness, my incessant nagging about helmets paid off, and they strapped them on.

Kristjana decided to show off and raced KC down the long, steep hill that was about a mile from our house.

Kristjana was in the lead. She was going too fast, so she pulled hard on her hand brakes. They didn't work. She pulled again, and they fell off the bike onto the road.

She lost control completely, hit the pavement face first, and skidded across the road. She lay there stunned but surprisingly quite calm—probably in shock.

KC screeched to a stop beside her and leaped off her bike.

"Kristjana, are you okay?"

"I hurt." Kristjana moaned.

"Can you sit up?"

"I think so."

Enter Briana. She took one look at Kristjana's face and started to cry and scream.

"Oh my gosh! Oh my gosh! You're gonna die!"

That did it. The entire western hemisphere heard the bellowing. The girls said it sounded like wild pigs stuck on the horns of a herd of mad bulls.

To this day, no one knows who called 911. Perhaps some neighbors grabbed their phones as they took shelter under their bed. Maybe the emergency response team heard her cry on the same channel Superman uses. All we know is that the ambulance mysteriously showed up and hightailed it to the hospital with Kristjana, sirens blasting.

The fact that I missed the entire kerfuffle is a testament to the noise level I was accustomed to in our home.

I had decided to take advantage of the few moments of alone time and indulge in an uninterrupted telephone call. That little miracle was not going to happen.

Briana came screaming into the house with KC and Amber on her heels.

"Kristjana's on her way to the hospital in the ambulance and, boy, is she a mess."

This was definitely a hang-up-the-phone emergency. I called Rick, but the hospital had already notified him at his office. He was likely filling jugs of water that very moment. We ran out the door and were almost in the car when my scrapbooking instincts clicked in.

"Briana, run back into the house and get the camera."

Rick was sitting beside Kristjana's bed holding her glass while she drank through a straw when we got to her room. She was trussed up in a whiplash collar and all her wounds were cleaned and dressed. Her face was a mass of sores that had started to swell. A tooth was knocked out, and her arms from the elbow down were all scraped up as well as her shins.

"Krissy, are you OK? What happened?" I rushed to her bed to hug and comfort her.

"Mother, please tell me you did not bring a camera."

"Of course I brought a camera. Don't you want to show your children what you looked like on the first big accident of your life?"

"What do you mean my first big accident?" She raised herself up on her elbow. "Are you trying to tell me I am going to have more of these?"

"Don't panic, sweetheart. I didn't mean it like that."

"You are not going to take my picture. Out of all the millions of mothers in the world, could I be blessed with one who's heard of conventional flowers or chocolates or cheerful balloons? No, my mom brings a camera. What, are you working for NBC now? Even a half-eaten peanut butter sandwich would be more thoughtful than your camera."

Someone in the room started to laugh.

"Aren't you going to tell me what happened? Does your face hurt?"

"Mom, are you blind? Of course it hurts. Yours would too if you flew off your bike and skidded on your face down a thousand miles of pavement."

For some reason that picture ran like a cartoon reel in my head. I could see an animation of Wile E. Coyote's face rolling up like a scroll as the pavement pushed out in front of him like a roll of Laffy Taffy.

What kind of mother was I? I tried to bite my lip and chew on my cheeks, but I burst out laughing anyway.

"Mother, it's not funny. There I was, swimming in a pool of my own blood, hurting, just glad to be alive when Briana comes up and freaks out. Her eyes bugged out like a horror movie frog monster and she starts screaming, 'You're gonna die! You're gonna die!' I thought I was roadkill."

Everyone was laughing by now.

"Ya'll need to stop laughing. I'm dying here."

I managed to compose myself enough to talk. "So, Kristjana, do you want to see your face?" I started to pull the mirror out of my purse.

"Mom, you are a regular Florence Nightingfail! I don't feel bad enough yet? Maybe you'd like to stab me in the heart. Do you have a knife in there too? Why don't you carve out my appendix while you're here? Of course I don't want to see my face. I'll see it later in your stupid picture."

By now, Briana and Amber were crying, KC was snorting, and Rick was gasping for breath as the drama queen lisped her tirade through the hole where a tooth used to be. Her face contorted in indignation.

I have often wondered why Kristjana didn't take up acting or at the very least write her own screenplays. The dialogue would be over the top.

The roadkill princess shook her head. "I can't believe you all find my near-death experience so hilarious." She held out her green puke container. "You can pay for the entertainment now."

When I could finally breathe, I gasped. "Ha, I heard you say I could take your picture."

"Well, yeah—later, maybe. I just don't want it now."

I pulled out the camera. "Kristjana you have to take a picture now. What's the point in taking one after you heal? Nobody will believe how awful you look."

"This moment just keeps getting better. Mom, do you even think before you speak? You are like a volcano. You just open your mouth and erupt."

"I didn't mean it like that. This picture will be like your own little badge of courage. You'll be able to show people how brave you were."

"D-a-a-d. Can't you stop her?"

Rick looked like a laughing Buddha, wheezing with laughter, the tears pouring down his cheeks. He couldn't speak.

Kristjana took one look at him and started to laugh. "All right, take your stupid picture already. But I don't want to see it for a month."

I took off the lens cap and zoomed in.

"Lift up your elbow so we can get the scratches under your arm. Good, turn your head to the right a little."

"Mother! I'm sorry my bloody carcass isn't laid out right for your picture.

"Good, open your mouth so I can see the missing tooth. Say *cheese* for posterity."

Kristjana curled her lip over the broken tooth and sneered. "Florence Nightingfail!"

Technically Speaking

A Dilemma is dropping your cell phone into the toilet. A crisis is when the toilet isn't flushed. A catastrophe is when there are no rubber gloves in the house.

The other day I had a catastrophe. All I could do was stand and stare at my cell phone. How had this happened?

Something like dropping your phone into the toilet would never have happened in the good old days when phones were bolted securely to the wall.

I have fond memories of a time when I had to actually run to the phone when it rang. On a good day, I could get all the aerobic exercise I needed just by running to answer it. Now all I have to do is click a little button attached to my ear.

Instead of getting my exercise by doing something that makes sense and moves me through my day, I now have to schedule time to drive to a park or a track where I run around in circles for an hour. And buy an expensive pair of shoes to do it.

I had about as much attachment to my first cell phone as I had for a pet rock. It was a hand-me-down, an antique. According to my children, it was so big it was like slamming a brick up to your head.

Since my children became teenagers, I've become well acquainted with the feeling of wanting to slam my head against a brick wall, so I figured I would get along quite well with their reject. However, I never considered the learning curve.

Even if I liked nothing better than reading a book of directions written in miniscule print, I had no time. All I wanted to know was how to make and receive calls. I called in the experts: my children.

Apparently communicating with their friends was worth working at McDonald's, and all of my children had their own phone. It was permanently attached to their ear, like a tumor, but I was finally able to pry Garret away from his social networking long enough to give me the basics on my prehistoric phone.

"Mom, you just push the buttons to dial and then push the green one to send. When it makes a noise, open it up, push the green button, and talk." Those were instructions I could understand, so I headed confidently to the grocery store.

A display of diet shakes at the end of one of the aisles caught my eye. I would be burning fewer calories now that I was carrying my own communication network, so I decided to check it out.

The instant I picked up a box to read the ingredients, music began to play. I'd never heard of musical diet shakes before. I needed to watch more TV and catch up on the new commercials.

Where was it coming from? I couldn't find it in the box I was holding, so I grabbed another one. I turned it upside down and sideways. The music kept playing. I put that box down and grabbed another then another. Nothing.

Maybe something was hidden in the center of the display. I started to dig into the middle of the boxes.

"Where the heck is that music coming from?" I said out loud. I quit digging, and the music immediately stopped.

Weird. It had to be a prank. I glanced around to see if I was being filmed on some reality show. I decided I may as well buy a box of the shakes. Maybe I'd find the secret of its music at home.

I picked up a box, and instantly the music started again. This time I was determined to find it. I ripped off the plastic and opened the package.

Suddenly it occurred to me that the noise was coming from my purse. I snatched it from my shoulder; dug around inside, found my phone, flipped it open, and pushed the green button.

"Hello! Rick, why didn't you call me before I left home so I knew what the ring was like? I've been doing a dummy dance with the diet drinks. You didn't tell me you changed the tune."

I was listening for the Snoopy Dog rapper ring Briana used. I was glad Rick changed it, but would it be too much to ask him to inform me?

Shortly after that humiliation, Jason upgraded his phone and gave me his hand-me-down. He now required a phone with a camera, a calculator, a wide screen TV, and a robot that vacuums while it makes lattes and yet is so small that it can be implanted under your left thumbnail. Since I have better things to do with my money, his old phone suited me fine.

I took it with me when I went out of town to visit a friend. After a crash course on using the directory and retrieving messages and missed calls, I was ready. Then I got on the plane.

"Please turn off your cell phones."

Uh-oh, I'd never been required to do that before. Which button did I push? I looked around, frantic. A kid across the aisle turned his off while his mother beamed and then handed him his Tickle Me Elmo. I am an idiot. Maybe I could leave it on. No, with my luck it would ring and I'd be hauled to some foreign prison. I had no choice. I looked at the woman sitting to my left and the gentleman on my right.

"Excuse me, sir," I flashed my best smile. "Could you please show me how to turn off my phone?"

The man was obviously shocked. I knew he wanted to tell me to crawl back to my cave and use two tin cans and a string. He pointed to a miniscule red button and coldly turned his back to me for the rest of the trip. I felt like I was the H1N1 virus.

The woman on my left consoled me, "It's a good thing you didn't ask me. I can't figure those things out either."

I gave up on cell phones for a while, but when it became evident that they were more than a passing fad, I caved and bought my own. I had just learned how to use voice mail too and now, here it was, taking its first swim in the toilet.

In our society, cleanliness is only a flush away, but someone in our house was flush handicapped, and I used the last of the latex gloves yesterday. How long could a cell phone last in the water? Was it dead already? Rick was home, but it wasn't like I could call out cheerfully and say, "Honey, would you mind digging my cell phone out of the toilet for me?"

Earlier that day he mentioned he needed a new phone. I suggested he get me an iPhone, and I could give him mine. Chances of that were now . . . yup, in the toilet.

Which item was more important? Hmmm, the cell phone kept me in touch with society while the toilet kept me from offending society. I couldn't live without either one!

At some point in time, flushing would be imminent. Our commode was a powerful flusher, and I risked losing the phone or, worse yet, it might get lodged in the toilet and not only would it flood but we might have to call the plumber to lift it up off the base to dislodge it. Maybe life would be simpler if I just took the next shuttle to the moon.

I remember a Christmas when we were at Rick's parents. They had a little nativity set Jason liked to play with. He was particularly fond of the baby Jesus and would often carry him around. One day we couldn't find the tiny figure. We searched for days.

About that same time the toilet started acting up. We had to plunge it several times a day. After a few days, Rick's dad rented a snake and stuck it inside the toilet to try to dislodge whatever was stuck. Finally they had to call the plumber, who had to take the toilet off the base. Lo and behold, lodged sideways was the missing baby Jesus; clean and undamaged.

I knelt by the toilet and dismally considered my prospects. Since a shuttle to the moon was not an option, I apologized to my hand, forced it into the murk, and pulled out my phone. I dashed over to the sink and scrubbed us both down with soap and hot water. If my phone wasn't dead before, it should be now.

I am proud to say that my technical skills are such that I can now use intelligent terms. Instead of saying I took the doohickey out of the thing-a-ma-bob, I can say I pried off the back and took out the SIM card. I gave it CPR with my blow dryer. I blew both sides, being careful not to melt any of the wires. When it seemed dry, I put it back together. It didn't work. There was only one thing to do.

When my sewing machine acts up and won't work, I turn it off and leave it alone. When I turn it on the next day, it works just fine. Maybe my phone had sewing machine parts.

I opened it up again, took the parts back out and left everything on the counter overnight. Sure enough, in the morning it worked perfectly.

Now I have a new dilemma: since my phone's little escapade, I am highly motivated to give it to Rick. However, what if I get an iPhone and drop it into the toilet?

I better stock up on rubber gloves, get a warranty, and call NASA.

culinary illiterate

culinary illiterate! If it sounds like a cuss word, it's supposed to.

I may not have known how to plunge a toilet when I got married, but I did know which end of the wok was up.

Rick claims the first dish I served him was pizza and it was like soup on a soggy crust. The man's a liar. I have no recollection of any such meal.

I had a passion for teaching my children to cook for many reasons. When we were in Iowa, a friend of mine was having company for dinner. Thank goodness, it wasn't Rick and me.

She had a reputation for her love of reading; too bad she never picked up a cookbook.

Corn happened to be on the menu that night. No arduous use of brain matter there. The problem was she had no more corn in the house. Had she cooked enough? Hmmm . . . what would a culinary illiterate do? Of course! Popcorn. It's just dehydrated corn, after all. It would soften up, and nobody would be the wiser. Thousands of dollars on dental work later . . .

The kitchen can be a dangerous place, where body parts can be sacrificed if you have no skills. I myself have come close to forfeiting a finger or two.

No matter how careful you are or how many times you have instructed your children, accidents will happen.

One day Jason decided to make macaroni and cheese in the pressure cooker. Twenty-five pots in the house, and he chose the pressure cooker. Yup, he took the lid off. It exploded. He screamed. Macaroni art took on a whole new meaning.

He spent spring break lying on the couch in bandages. When he went back to school, they thought he had been abused and almost called Child Protective Services.

I felt obligated to teach Adam to cook a little earlier than my other children because he turned out to have such deplorable manners.

One day he called my friend Sue and invited himself to dinner. She told him she really hadn't thought about dinner yet and her family would probably just eat leftovers.

That didn't bother my Adam. "That's okay." he said. "If you have some of that dessert you served yesterday, I could just eat the rest of that."

I realized if he didn't have something to offer he might never be invited out into polite society again, so I taught him to make cookies. It worked. He made the best cookies ever, and his friends' parents would invite him over for the afternoon to make cookies for them. Cookies saved him from being a social outcast.

Then there are the true culinary illiterates. These are the children of whom society will surely say, "Poor things, their mother must have died at childbirth."

That would describe my niece Tyna and my daughter Briana.

Tyna was sucking on an ice cube one day when suddenly she made an exciting discovery. Her "Aha moment" was much like Archimedes when he discovered the principle of water displacement and shouted, "Eureka!" How appropriate that her find involved water too.

"Wow," she said. "So that's how they make ice. It's only water!"

Who'd have thunk it—my niece and Archimedes. I wish I could compare Briana to a brilliant scientist.

I don't know if you watched the news one long-ago day, but if you go back in history, I am sure you will find this headline in newspapers all over the world: FISH FLYING IN SKY OVER WASHINGTON STATE.

That was the day that Briana, who absolutely refused to cook because she was going to marry a chef, decided to bake a cake.

My heart was palpating to the beat of "Zip-a-dee-doo-dah, Zip-a-dee-ay" while my brain was singing "Nothing Is Impossible."

I danced over to the cookbook. "Pick out any cake you want, my darling daughter."

"Mom, it's me, Briana. I'm talking mix here. You do have one, don't you?"

My musical concerto slowed down a little, but hey, it was a start.

"Chocolate, white, or spice?" I sang.

She grabbed for the chocolate one. "Will you help me?"

"Briana, they have directions on the back and pictures. You can do this all by yourself."

I pinched her cheek and burst out with a few words to one of my favorite show tunes. "I have confidence in confidence alone." And adapted the words from another movie, "No shilly shallying, no dilly dallying, you can make a cake right now." I ended on one knee on the floor with my arms thrown out to the sides.

She started to laugh. "Okay, Mother. I think I'd like to be alone now. But don't go far."

"You'll be fine. After all, you can read, you know."

What I didn't realize was that the words she read vanished from her thoughts and roamed around in what I can only assume is a very lonely room in her brain.

A little bit later she called. "Mom, how am I supposed to beat this batter?"

"Use the eggbeaters."

"Mom, I need you. How do I get the beaters in here?"

"Briana," I walked back into the room. "You put them into the hole on the bottom of the egg beater."

She looked at the beaters and at the box. "I know that. How do you fit them into the box?"

That effectively shut me up until I had time to compute the fact that she had added all the ingredients *into the box*.

"Briana, what are you thinking?" She had dumped the oil, eggs, and some of the water into the box. "You are supposed to dump the cake mix into a bowl and then add the ingredients."

"You told me to follow the directions. Nowhere on this box does it say to dump the cake mix into a bowl."

Was I supposed to laugh or cry—or scream while I ripped my hair out?

"Briana! Common sense. How did you figure you were going to get the egg beaters into the box?"

"Duh, that's why I called you."

Well, how could I have been so dumb?

You would have thought after an experience like that, I would never have trusted Briana in the kitchen again. However, desperate times . . .

"Briana, this is an emergency. Who else is home besides you?"

"No one, Mom. What's up?"

"No one else is there?"

"Nope."

"OK, pay attention. We are having company come for dinner. I'm bringing home a chicken, but I need you to turn the oven on to 375 degrees. Go do it now."

I wasn't taking any chances. She did it and then asked, "Now what?"

"Get eight potatoes, poke holes in them with a fork, and put them on the top rack of the oven. You got that?"

"Are you sure you want potatoes?"

"Of course I'm sure. What else would I bake?"

"Okay," she said dubiously.

"Do it right now and poke lots of holes in them. We'll be there in a little while."

We arrived about an hour later. I hurried to check the oven. I couldn't believe my eyes. When I finally got the power of speech back, I yelled. "Briana—*potatoes*! I said *potatoes*. Have I even once in my entire life ever baked *tomatoes*?"

I made the mistake of telling my dad about his brilliant progeny. He flew into such an apoplectic rage, I immediately got on the phone and advised Briana and Tyna to flee the country.

Briana was pretty much banned from the kitchen after that. I am not sure if she is safe with any appliance except her curling iron and blow dryer.

I am making my public appeal in her behalf now. If there are any handsome, rich chefs who want to marry an adorable airhead, she comes with a great dowry: a mother with a fabulous sense of humor.

ATTACK OF THE KILLER MASCARA

C-O-O-L; you've either got it or you don't. I grew up in a small town in Southern Alberta, and somehow I was always on the fringes of the cool crowd. I moved to Cardston at the end of first grade, so when they had elections in kindergarten to determine who those anointed few would be, I missed out.

I was shallow back then, and my main goal in life was to be cool. I was determined to follow all the rules that the leaders of the "cool" kingdom wrote, no matter how much suffering it required.

That meant rolling my skirt up past my knees the moment I was a block away from my house. Even if I had to walk the eight blocks to school in temperatures that would make living at the North Pole feel like Miami Beach.

Some days my legs were so frozen I had to be careful not to bang them against the desk for fear of chipping them.

We were not allowed to wear pants to school unless we took them off when we got there. Cool people would rather amputate frozen limbs.

However, wearing pants under your dress would render you much less of a social pariah than to commit the unpardonable social gaffe of carrying an umbrella. I don't care if it rained so hard that you arrived at school looking like you had just swum the English Channel, the "cool" did not carry an umbrella.

It's sad to have to admit it, but when something even that ridiculous is so entwined in the patterning of your brain, it is hard to wrench loose. Even when I traveled to Europe and saw everyone carry umbrellas with a debonair flair, it was too late. I was brainwashed for life.

Then I moved to the Pacific Northwest, where it rains ten months of the year. I held onto my honor for twelve years until the inevitable happened and I became an umbrella convert.

One warm day in my preumbrella era, I was innocently strolling the four miles to work at my husband's office when it started to rain. It was just a drizzle, but after I walked about half a mile, I could not see.

I knew I was about a couple of blocks away from the Meyers' house, but my eyes were burning so badly I had to close them. Was this what they meant by acid rain?

What I wouldn't have given for a seeing-eye dog. I would even have put up with a Saint Bernard knocking me over and drowning me in slobber if he could lead me safely to her house.

I leaned my head as far back as I could and tried to squint through my drippy lashes. I scanned the area directly in front of me, closed my eyes, stumbled forward a few steps, and then opened them again to search for the next landmark.

Groping my way, I managed to creep to her door and ring the bell. My eyes were shut, so I couldn't see who answered, but I knew it was one of her children when they slammed the door in my face and hollered,

"Mom, there's a monster at the door." It was close to Halloween, after all.

I was insulted that Juanne recognized me. She didn't seem a bit surprised to see me standing on her porch with my hair slicked to my head and black streaks dripping from my chin.

She led me to the bathroom, gave me a facecloth, and then called Rick. I let him know I needed a ride because I had been attacked by my mascara. During that defining moment, I lost my cool. I would be buying an umbrella.

If I was going to step into the world of the geek, it would be with class. I ransacked several stores, casting aside polka dots, flowers, geometric, and paisley designs before I found an umbrella with the perfect personality.

There she stood, aloof and unique, a beautiful tan with black on the underside and a long handle that gently turned into an ebony curve at the end. I became so attached, I named her.

Eunice became the object of a new set of worries. She was so beautiful. What if I left her unattended in an umbrella stand somewhere and a stranger stole her? What if someone wanted to borrow her and she broke?

My children were constantly trying to sneak her out the door, but I found a place where I could keep my eye on her. Her ebony handle hooked behind my favorite chair, where I could see her at all times.

One day I left to go grocery shopping, and the sun was shining. I was optimistic, so I gave Eunice a fond gaze and set out alone.

I was ready to leave the store when the downpour started. I was with a large group of women gathered by the glass exit. They all stood there, wondering how to proceed. Where was Eunice when I needed her? I had an appointment in ten minutes but waited a bit to see if the rain would quit.

The deluge was not letting up. What would MacGyver do? I scoped out the vicinity to see what resources were available. Aha! I whipped open a plastic grocery bag, pulled it over my head, and grabbed the handles under my chin. A stream of laughter followed me as I ran into the pouring rain—the cowards. They obviously knew nothing about cool.

The bag quickly became drenched and pushed down over my face. They might have found me suffocated and drowning right there in the parking lot with that bag on my head if I hadn't finally remembered where I parked my car.

I bent over to pack in the groceries. Did I care that my back side was getting soaked? Absolutely not. I was only concerned about my head. It's not just the hair. It's the makeup. Until you've been attacked by killer mascara, you will never understand.

WHEN PIGS FLY

"WATCH OUT FOR FLYING PIGS TODAY, HON."

"What are you talking about?" Rick opened one eye. "What time is it?"

"It's 5:00. I've decided this year, we are going to have a garden."

"Don't torture me this early in the morning. Last year you planted all the tulip bulbs upside down, remember?"

I jabbed him hard in the ribs. "I'm talking about a vegetable garden this time. The seeds only go into the ground one direction. It'll be fun and educational for the kids."

"Ummmm," he rolled over. "Tell me about it in the morning."

I jumped out of bed and got to work. A garden would be the perfect bonding experience. The kids would learn a lot about responsibility and the joy of growing their own food.

I had learned many life skills through gardening: how to deck whining brothers who lied about working harder than I did, the art of throwing dirt clods like projectile missiles, and the ins and outs of the emergency room.

Isn't it a parent's job to give their children the opportunity to hate the things they hated as a child? It's good for their character. Besides, I didn't want them to grow up thinking food came from paper bags that sprouted every few days in the back seat of the car.

There was no place at our house for a garden, so we rented a community plot.

G-day arrived, and Rick suddenly developed a weak back and bad knees while the boys decided character was overrated and they had all they needed. The only interest they had in food during the summer was the immediate gratification that was served up at the ice-cream truck. The girls and I headed off on our adventure and drove the five miles to the little piece of green acres we would be sharing.

Who were these people? Their gardens looked as if the gardener for the Queen of England had personally manicured them. The rows were all marked and straight, plants were already poking their heads up, with nary a weed in sight. I felt like we were the Beverly Hillbillies trashing up the neighborhood.

We got out of the car and began schlepping manure—lots of manure, sweet-smelling, fresh from the barnyard manure—and fertilized our little spot of Eden.

Then we hauled out the tools: a rusty shovel, a bent hoe, our rake with the two bent prongs, and the garden hose.

Gardening had changed in the last twenty years. The directions on the seed packets were miniscule, and the ground was a lot farther away.

Ariana read the directions. Perfect! We forgot to bring the measuring tape. Just how deep was ¼–½ an inch, and how were we supposed to get our rows straight? We found a couple of old sticks across the street and some string in the car and eyeballed it.

We scattered carrots, peas, beets, onions, lettuce, and radishes in the rows, planted our tomato plants, and then packed up our tools.

We rushed back a few days later, excited to see if anything was up. Our seeds obviously did not have the super growth hormone of our neighbors' gardens. We watered and went away for another week. One day, little green sprouts poked their little happy heads out of the dirt. We knelt down to ooh and aah.

"So Mom, which ones are the weeds?" asked Kristjana.

I looked around at the neighboring plots. "Bite your tongue. We're not allowed to have weeds. It will anger the natives."

"The ones growing in rows will be the plants and the others will be weeds, doofus," Ariana said. Kristjana picked up a dry piece of manure and threw it at her.

Aww, just like the good old days, I thought.

"I used to be able to tell which ones were plants. There's the package for carrots and peas. Let's look at it. Maybe they have a picture."

"Mom, the plants are so tiny. This will take all day."

This from Briana, who loved her new gardening gloves but hated the idea of actually mucking them up.

It looked like a lot of work to me too, so I did the adult thing—I decided to wait until they got a little bigger and we could get in there with the hoe. When they got bigger, I reasoned, we could see what they were.

We watered and gave it another week. A week didn't do much. We could find the carrots, but they were so tiny that it would be too easy to pick them when we went in after the weeds, so we decided to water and come back after vacation.

I've read the Bible, and I knew that a lot happened over a period of one day in the Garden of Eden. I mean things—*really* changed. So, I shouldn't have been surprised by what happened to our little piece of Eden the week we were gone on vacation. It looked like the devil himself had paid it a visit.

I thought maybe I should get up enough nerve to ask my mother-in-law, who was here visiting, to come help us tell the weeds from the plants. Yeah, like that would happen. Now was not the time to inform the lady with ten green fingers and a green toe that I was too dumb to know a weed from a plant.

I had mentioned our problem to Rick, but he was as interested as he would be in an insect bite. I wanted to impress upon him the fact that our little garden cost us more in seed, fertilizer, and gardening gloves than we were likely to see in food production if he didn't help us, but that would have been just plain crazy.

We were too busy to do more than throw a little water on the garden after vacation, and it wasn't until several days later that we drove out with our rusty tools and our virgin gardening gloves. The weeds were about knee high by now.

"Girls, these people look hostile. We can't go clean up the garden now. Scrunch down in the seat. We don't want them to know who we are." I pulled my own hat down and slid low behind the wheel.

For thirty minutes, we circled the block. Multitudes of green thumbers were nurturing their royal gardens, pausing only to shake a hoe or rake violently in the direction of our weedy showcase.

Later that night, we snuck back to weed the garden. We had duct taped flashlights to our foreheads. We needed both hands free to attack any plant that looked suspicious. We were on a mission.

Was it possible that our primitive miner hats weren't bright enough to see the weeds? We bent our head lower. Our garden was gone! Plowed up! Every single plant, even the rows we had tried to weed. The only survivors were our caged tomato plants.

Who did this? It couldn't have been the city. Since when do they act so quickly? We didn't get a notice. Not even a stick shoved in the ground with a scrap of paper saying, "Your Garden Stinks."

The villagers must have complained that we were bringing down the property values. I could picture them, picketing the mayor and city council, waving pitchforks and lanterns, demanding immediate action.

There was only one thing to do. Dig up our tomato plants and never show our face in the neighborhood again.

On second thought, maybe we should call 911.

HAPPY MOTHER'S DAZE!

ABOUT THE AUTHOR

Jane is married to Rick Still, who she believes has the distinction of being the only man in history brave enough to give her earwax candles for her birthday. They had six children in eight years, and while her children were growing up, she discovered she had a great sense of humor. At least that was her take. Rick once said to her, "Honey, you know all those real corny things you say all the time? Who ever thought you could make money at it?" Her son Adam once told her, "Mom could you please stop telling jokes to my friends? It's really embarrassing." One of Jane's philosophies is, "You're not doing your job unless your children are worried about being seen in public with you."

To read more about Jane and her exploits, visit her website at **www.janeisfeldstill.com** or her blog at **www.janeisfeldstill.blogspot.com**.

0 26575 54952 2